CHECKERBOARD BIOGRAPHY LIBRARY

U.S. PRESIDENTS

The
United States Presidents

JIMMY CARTER

ABDO Publishing Company

Heidi M.D. Elston

visit us at
www.abdopublishing.com

Published by ABDO Publishing Company, 8000 West 78th Street, Edina, Minnesota 55439.
Copyright © 2009 by Abdo Consulting Group, Inc. International copyrights reserved in all
countries. No part of this book may be reproduced in any form without written permission from the
publisher. The Checkerboard Library™ is a trademark and logo of ABDO Publishing Company.

Printed in the United States.

Cover Photo: Getty Images
Interior Photos: AP Images p. 15; The Carter Center p. 27; Corbis pp. 5, 9, 13, 17, 20;
    Getty Images p. 23; iStockphoto p. 32; Courtesy: Jimmy Carter Library pp. 10, 11, 14, 22, 25;
    Library of Congress p. 19; National Park Service p. 8; Picture History p. 21;
    Rick Diamond/The Carter Center p. 29; Stephen Cord/The Carter Center p. 28

Editor: BreAnn Rumsch
Art Direction & Cover Design: Neil Klinepier
Interior Design: Jaime Martens

Library of Congress Cataloging-in-Publication Data

Elston, Heidi M. D., 1979-
  Jimmy Carter / Heidi M.D. Elston.
    p. cm. -- (United States presidents)
  Includes index.
  ISBN 978-1-60453-445-0
  1. Carter, Jimmy, 1924---Juvenile literature. 2. Presidents--United States--Biography--Juvenile
literature. I. Title.

  E873.E47 2009
  973.926092--dc22
  [B]
                            2008041628

CONTENTS

JIMMY CARTER

In November 1976, Jimmy Carter was elected the thirty-ninth U.S. president. Because of recent government **scandals**, many Americans were looking for a change. Carter's main goal was to return honor and pride to the president's office.

Carter emphasized morality in government. He also believed the government should help the poor and the needy. Voters trusted Carter and felt comfortable with him. He was a simple man from a small farm town in the Deep South.

At the time Carter became president, the U.S. **economy** was in trouble. Prices of food, gas, and many other items people needed to live were rising. Buying a house was hard, and saving for the future was even harder.

As his presidency was nearing a close, Carter ran for reelection. But, many people blamed him for the country's economic problems. So he lost the election.

Today, Carter continues to give back to his country. He remains an image of honor and pride in America.

TIMELINE

1924 - On October 1, James Earl Carter Jr. was born in Plains, Georgia.

1946 - Carter graduated from the U.S. Naval Academy in Annapolis, Maryland; on July 7, he married Eleanor Rosalynn Smith.

1953 - Carter quit the navy.

1963 - On January 14, Carter took office as a Georgia state senator.

1964 - Carter was reelected to the Georgia state senate.

1970 - Carter was elected governor of Georgia.

1974 - On December 12, Carter announced his candidacy for president.

1977 - Carter took office as the thirty-ninth U.S. president on January 20; he asked Congress to pass the Emergency Natural Gas Act.

1978 - Carter made history by arranging a meeting between Israeli prime minister Menachem Begin and Egyptian president Anwar Sadat; the U.S. Senate approved two treaties regarding the Panama Canal.

1979 - On November 4, more than 50 Americans were taken hostage in Iran.

1980 - Carter lost his bid for reelection to Ronald Reagan.

1982 - Mr. and Mrs. Carter founded The Carter Center in Atlanta, Georgia.

1986 - The Carter Presidential Center was dedicated in Atlanta.

1999 - Mr. and Mrs. Carter each received the Presidential Medal of Freedom.

2002 - Carter received the Nobel Peace Prize.

Jimmy Carter was the first president born in a hospital.

From a young age, Carter knew he wanted to join the navy. He thought his feet were flat and worried the U.S. Naval Academy wouldn't accept him. So, he rolled his feet over Coke bottles to strengthen his arches.

Carter was a speed-reader. He could read 2,000 words per minute!

Carter was the first U.S. Naval Academy graduate to become a U.S. president.

Carter was the first president to walk with his family from his inauguration ceremony at the U.S. Capitol to the White House.

LITTLE JIMMY

James Earl Carter Jr. was born on October 1, 1924, in Plains, Georgia. His whole life he has gone by Jimmy. Jimmy was the oldest son of James Earl Carter Sr. and Lillian Gordy Carter. He had two sisters, Gloria and Ruth. His brother was named William. The family called him Billy. Jimmy's father was called Earl. Earl was a farmer and a businessman. He grew corn, cotton, and peanuts. Earl also operated a small general store in Archery, Georgia.

Lillian Gordy Carter and James Earl Carter Sr.

FAST FACTS

BORN - October 1, 1924
WIFE - Eleanor Rosalynn Smith (1927–)
CHILDREN - 4
POLITICAL PARTY - Democrat
AGE AT INAUGURATION - 52
YEARS SERVED - 1977–1981
VICE PRESIDENT - Walter Mondale

Lillian, Jimmy's mother, was a registered nurse. She was a caring, giving woman. Often, she helped patients without receiving any pay. Lillian also loved to read books and travel.

The Carter family moved to Archery when Jimmy was four. There, they lived in a small house without plumbing or electricity. They were members of the Plains Baptist Church. Religion, education, and hard work were important to the family.

Jimmy began his business career at a young age. When he was only five, he began selling boiled peanuts. On weekdays, Jimmy earned one dollar a day. He made about five dollars on Saturdays!

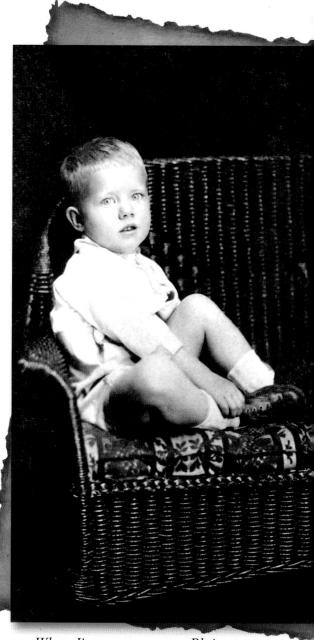

When Jimmy was young, Plains was a small town. Only about 600 people lived there.

A Dream Fulfilled

Jimmy attended public schools in nearby Plains. He was a good student. His favorite subjects were history, literature, and music. And like his mother, Jimmy loved to read. He even belonged to a book lovers' club. Jimmy graduated high school at the top of his class. He was the first member of his family to graduate from high school.

In 1941, Jimmy attended Georgia Southwestern College in Americus. The next year, he entered the Georgia Institute of Technology in Atlanta.

Jimmy fulfilled a childhood dream in 1943. That year, he entered the U.S. Naval Academy in Annapolis, Maryland. Jimmy was an excellent student. He liked military studies and training. In 1946, Jimmy graduated fifty-ninth in a class of 820.

Jimmy's first naval assignment was on the USS Wyoming *out of Norfolk, Virginia.*

The year before his graduation, Jimmy had started dating his sister Ruth's best friend. Eleanor Rosalynn Smith, known as Rosalynn, was also from Plains. Jimmy married Rosalynn on July 7, 1946.

Jimmy spent more than six years as a naval officer. In 1948, he was accepted for submarine duty. Jimmy quickly moved up the ranks. His naval career seemed promising. Then tragedy struck, and Jimmy's plans changed instantly.

Mr. and Mrs. Carter were married at Plains Methodist Church.

FAMILY MAN

In 1953, James Earl Carter Sr. died. At that time, he was a member of the Georgia House of Representatives. People throughout the state were saddened by his death.

Carter saw how his father had touched people's lives. He decided he wanted to model his life after his father's. So, Carter quit the navy later that year. Then, he returned to Plains.

In Plains, Carter worked hard to make the family farm and peanut business successful. He also became involved in local government. Carter served on the school board. He was also a member of the library and hospital boards.

Carter tried to **integrate** schools and churches in the area. But, many of his neighbors did not agree with his views on racial issues. So Carter's efforts failed.

By this time, the Carters had three sons. John William "Jack" had been born in 1947. James Earl III "Chip" followed in 1950. And, Donnel Jeffrey "Jeff" had been born in 1952. The Carters had their daughter, Amy Lynn, in 1967.

Mr. and Mrs. Carter (center) with their extended family

STOPPING VOTER FRAUD

In 1962, Carter sought the **Democratic** nomination for the Georgia state senate. He lost the **primary** election to Homer Moore by just 139 votes. Carter believed Moore had won because of **fraud**. So, he fought the election results and requested the votes be recounted.

After the recount, Carter was declared the winner of the primary. He had just three days to prepare for the general election! Still, Carter won by about 1,000 votes.

On January 14, 1963, Carter took office. As a state senator, he watched over the budget and did not waste money. Carter also promoted programs that helped the poor. And, he fought for education reforms. People loved his ideas. They reelected Carter to the Georgia state senate in 1964.

14

Carter (fourth from left) being sworn into the Georgia state senate

GOVERNOR CARTER

In 1966, Carter announced he would run for governor of Georgia. However, he did not win the **Democratic** nomination. Carter wasn't discouraged. Right away, he made plans to run again in four years.

Carter was elected governor of Georgia in 1970. His term began the next year on January 12. Carter was different from most southern governors at that time. He supported **integration**. And, he appointed many African Americans to state government jobs.

As governor, Carter made a series of reforms. One new law provided equal state aid to schools in wealthy and poor areas. Carter also passed laws to protect the **environment** and preserve historic sites.

Governor Carter traveled often. He also welcomed many international visitors. And, he met with leading national politicians. Carter believed he would make an able president. So on December 12, 1974, Carter announced he would run for president.

Lillian Carter recalled learning of her son's desire to run for president in 1973. He told her, "Momma, I'm going to run for president of the United States, and I'm going to win."

WATERGATE SCANDAL

Meanwhile, a political **scandal** called Watergate had rocked the country. Americans were left with a distrust for their government. The scandal is named after the Watergate office **complex** in Washington, D.C.

There, police arrested five men on June 17, 1972. The men had broken into the **Democratic National Committee** headquarters. They were there to steal secrets to help **Republican** president Richard Nixon's reelection campaign.

About 40 people were charged with crimes in relation to the scandal. These included several top White House aides. For months, President Nixon denied involvement in the break-in or the cover-up that followed. Yet on August 9, 1974, he left office.

That day, Vice President Gerald Ford became the thirty-eighth U.S. president. He stated, "Our long national nightmare is over." One month later, Ford pardoned Nixon. This meant that any crimes Nixon may have committed were forgiven. As a result, Ford's popularity dropped. This would help Carter in the next presidential election.

Nixon defended himself during the Watergate investigation, declaring "I am not a crook."

THE 1976 ELECTION

The 1976 **Democratic National Convention** was held in New York City, New York. There, party leaders chose Carter as their candidate for president. U.S. senator Walter Mondale was named his **running mate**. The **Republican** Party nominated President Ford. He chose Senator Bob Dole as his running mate.

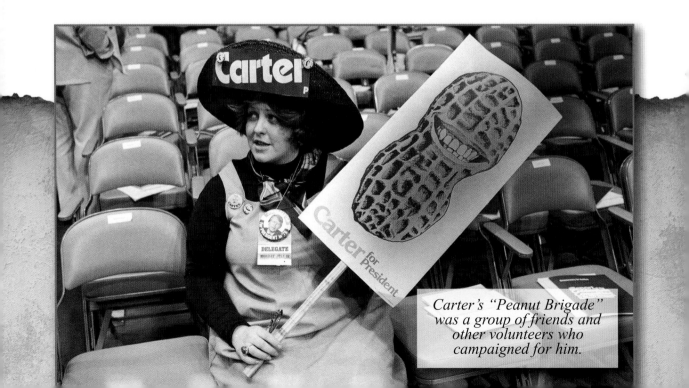

Carter's "Peanut Brigade" was a group of friends and other volunteers who campaigned for him.

Carter was not well-known. But, he appealed to many different kinds of people. Carter campaigned as an honest and trustworthy man. He pledged to create more jobs. He also promised to reorganize the federal government. Many men had avoided the **draft**

The 1976 election was very close. It wasn't until 3:30 AM that Carter knew he had won.

during the **Vietnam War**. Carter declared he would consider granting pardons to them.

The 1976 election for president was the closest in more than 60 years. On November 2, Carter won a narrow victory. He earned 297 electoral votes, while Ford received 240 votes.

RUNNING THE COUNTRY

On January 20, 1977, Carter was **inaugurated** the thirty-ninth U.S. president. One of Carter's first acts as president fulfilled a campaign promise. He pardoned those who had avoided the **draft** during the **Vietnam War**.

Carter took office during one of the worst winters in U.S. history. Because the weather was so cold, people used a lot of natural gas for heat. This caused a natural gas shortage. So, Carter asked Congress to pass the Emergency Natural Gas Act. This plan sent natural gas to areas of the country with severe shortages.

Another concern was the U.S. **economy**. Many Americans were without jobs. And prices for food, clothes, houses, and other basic necessities were high. President Carter focused on improving the economy. But, expenses continued to increase. As a result, Carter's popularity fell.

Joan and Walter Mondale with Rosalynn and Jimmy Carter

PRESIDENT CARTER'S CABINET

JANUARY 20, 1977–
JANUARY 20, 1981

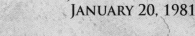

- **STATE –** Cyrus Vance
  Edmund S. Muskie (from May 8, 1980)
- **TREASURY –** W. Michael Blumenthal
  George W. Miller (from August 6, 1979)
- **DEFENSE –** Harold Brown
- **ATTORNEY GENERAL –** Griffin B. Bell
  Benjamin R. Civiletti (from August 16, 1979)
- **INTERIOR –** Cecil Dale Andrus
- **AGRICULTURE –** Robert S. Bergland
- **COMMERCE –** Juanita M. Kreps
  Philip M. Klutznick (from January 9, 1980)
- **LABOR –** F. Ray Marshall
- **HEALTH, EDUCATION, AND WELFARE –**
  Joseph A. Califano Jr.
  Patricia Roberts Harris (from August 3, 1979)
- **HEALTH AND HUMAN SERVICES –**
  Patricia Roberts Harris (from September 27, 1979)
- **HOUSING AND URBAN DEVELOPMENT –**
  Patricia Roberts Harris
  Moon Landrieu (from September 24, 1979)
- **TRANSPORTATION –** Brock Adams
  Neil E. Goldschmidt (from September 24, 1979)
- **ENERGY –** James R. Schlesinger (from October 1, 1977)
  Charles W. Duncan Jr. (from August 24, 1979)
- **EDUCATION –** Shirley M. Hufstedler (from December 6, 1979)

FOREIGN AFFAIRS

President Carter had better success helping other countries. He participated in **summit** meetings in Europe and Japan. He also traveled to South America, Africa, Asia, and the Middle East. There, he promoted world peace.

In 1978, President Carter made history. He conducted a meeting between Israeli prime minister Menachem Begin and Egyptian president Anwar Sadat. The two leaders agreed to create a peace treaty. Egypt and Israel adopted the treaty the following year.

Also in 1978, the U.S. Senate approved two treaties related to the **Panama Canal**. The United States had controlled the canal since the early 1900s. One treaty granted control of the canal to Panama by the year 2000. The second treaty allowed the United States to defend the canal's **neutrality**.

Then trouble struck. On November 4, 1979, the U.S. **embassy** in Iran was seized. More than 50 Americans were taken as **hostages**. Carter tried to arrange their release. However, they were not freed until moments after Carter left office in 1981.

Problems with Iran and the U.S. **economy** hurt Carter's chances for reelection. In November 1980, **Republican** Ronald Reagan defeated Carter. Carter received just 49 electoral votes. Reagan won 489.

On March 26, 1979, Sadat (left), *Carter, and Begin* (right) *celebrated the signing of the peace treaty between Egypt and Israel.*

A True Leader

After leaving the White House, Carter returned to Plains. He has remained active in retirement. Carter served as a professor at Emory University in Atlanta, Georgia. He also wrote more than 20 books.

Mr. and Mrs. Carter founded The Carter Center in 1982. It is based in Atlanta. The center works to resolve conflict throughout the world. It also fights disease, poverty, and hunger.

In 1986, the Carter Presidential Center **complex** was **dedicated**. Located in Atlanta, it includes The Carter Center and the Jimmy Carter Library and Museum.

The National Park Service manages the Jimmy Carter National Historic Site. It is located in Plains. The site is open to those interested in learning more about the former president.

Carter still travels to many countries. He promotes world peace and helps solve world problems. He also does much volunteer work. One week each year, Carter and his wife help with Habitat for Humanity. This organization helps needy people build homes for themselves.

Carter continues to travel around the world to promote good health.

Carter allows time for recreation, too. He enjoys fly-fishing, skiing, woodworking, bicycling, and playing tennis. Carter also teaches Sunday school at the Maranatha Baptist Church in Plains.

In 1999, Mr. and Mrs. Carter each received the Presidential Medal of Freedom. This is the nation's highest honor for nonmilitary people. Then in 2002, Carter received the Nobel Peace Prize. Each year, this prize is awarded to a person who works for world peace.

Carter worked hard for many years and accomplished much. He had an excellent career in the U.S. Navy. And, he turned a small peanut farm into a successful business. Carter advanced faster in politics than he did in the navy. In less than 20 years in elected office, Carter became president of the United States.

Carter is devoted to human rights and world peace.

Carter always did things the right way. He never took shortcuts and always worked honestly. From naval officer to president, he truly led by example. Today, Jimmy Carter remains a leader. Through volunteer work, he continues to promote a better world for all people.

OFFICE OF THE PRESIDENT

BRANCHES OF GOVERNMENT

The U.S. government is divided into three branches. They are the executive, legislative, and judicial branches. This division is called a separation of powers. Each branch has some power over the others. This is called a system of checks and balances.

EXECUTIVE BRANCH

The executive branch enforces laws. It is made up of the president, the vice president, and the president's cabinet. The president represents the United States around the world. He or she oversees relations with other countries and signs treaties. The president signs bills into law and appoints officials and federal judges. He or she also leads the military and manages government workers.

LEGISLATIVE BRANCH

The legislative branch makes laws, maintains the military, and regulates trade. It also has the power to declare war. This branch consists of the Senate and the House of Representatives. Together, these two houses make up Congress. Each state has two senators. A state's population determines the number of representatives it has.

JUDICIAL BRANCH

The judicial branch interprets laws. It consists of district courts, courts of appeals, and the Supreme Court. District courts try cases. If a person disagrees with a trial's outcome, he or she may appeal. If the courts of appeals support the ruling, a person may appeal to the Supreme Court. The Supreme Court also makes sure that laws follow the U.S. Constitution.

QUALIFICATIONS FOR OFFICE

To be president, a person must meet three requirements. A candidate must be at least 35 years old and a natural-born U.S. citizen. He or she must also have lived in the United States for at least 14 years.

ELECTORAL COLLEGE

The U.S. presidential election is an indirect election. Voters from each state choose electors to represent them in the Electoral College. The number of electors from each state is based on population. Each elector has one electoral vote. Electors are pledged to cast their vote for the candidate who receives the highest number of popular votes in their state. A candidate must receive the majority of Electoral College votes to win.

TERM OF OFFICE

Each president may be elected to two four-year terms. Sometimes, a president may only be elected once. This happens if he or she served more than two years of the previous president's term.

The presidential election is held on the Tuesday after the first Monday in November. The president is sworn in on January 20 of the following year. At that time, he or she takes the oath of office:

I do solemnly swear (or affirm) that I will faithfully execute the office of President of the United States, and will to the best of my ability, preserve, protect and defend the Constitution of the United States.

LINE OF SUCCESSION

The Presidential Succession Act of 1947 defines who becomes president if the president cannot serve. The vice president is first in the line of succession. Next are the Speaker of the House and the President Pro Tempore of the Senate. If none of these individuals is able to serve, the office falls to the president's cabinet members. They would take office in the order in which each department was created:

Secretary of State

Secretary of the Treasury

Secretary of Defense

Attorney General

Secretary of the Interior

Secretary of Agriculture

Secretary of Commerce

Secretary of Labor

Secretary of Health and Human Services

Secretary of Housing and Urban Development

Secretary of Transportation

Secretary of Energy

Secretary of Education

Secretary of Veterans Affairs

Secretary of Homeland Security

BENEFITS

- While in office, the president receives a salary of $400,000 each year. He or she lives in the White House and has 24-hour Secret Service protection.

- The president may travel on a Boeing 747 jet called Air Force One. The airplane can accommodate 70 passengers. It has kitchens, a dining room, sleeping areas, and a conference room. It also has fully equipped offices with the latest communications systems. Air Force One can fly halfway around the world before needing to refuel. It can even refuel in flight!

- If the president wishes to travel by car, he or she uses Cadillac One. Cadillac One is a Cadillac Deville. It has been modified with heavy armor and communications systems. The president takes Cadillac One along when visiting other countries if secure transportation will be needed.

- The president also travels on a helicopter called Marine One. Like the presidential car, Marine One accompanies the president when traveling abroad if necessary.

- Sometimes, the president needs to get away and relax with family and friends. Camp David is the official presidential retreat. It is located in the cool, wooded mountains in Maryland. The U.S. Navy maintains the retreat, and the U.S. Marine Corps keeps it secure. The camp offers swimming, tennis, golf, and hiking.

- When the president leaves office, he or she receives Secret Service protection for ten more years. He or she also receives a yearly pension of $191,300 and funding for office space, supplies, and staff.

PRESIDENTS AND THEIR TERMS

PRESIDENT	PARTY	TOOK OFFICE	LEFT OFFICE	TERMS SERVED	VICE PRESIDENT
George Washington	None	April 30, 1789	March 4, 1797	Two	John Adams
John Adams	Federalist	March 4, 1797	March 4, 1801	One	Thomas Jefferson
Thomas Jefferson	Democratic-Republican	March 4, 1801	March 4, 1809	Two	Aaron Burr, George Clinton
James Madison	Democratic-Republican	March 4, 1809	March 4, 1817	Two	George Clinton, Elbridge Gerry
James Monroe	Democratic-Republican	March 4, 1817	March 4, 1825	Two	Daniel D. Tompkins
John Quincy Adams	Democratic-Republican	March 4, 1825	March 4, 1829	One	John C. Calhoun
Andrew Jackson	Democrat	March 4, 1829	March 4, 1837	Two	John C. Calhoun, Martin Van Buren
Martin Van Buren	Democrat	March 4, 1837	March 4, 1841	One	Richard M. Johnson
William H. Harrison	Whig	March 4, 1841	April 4, 1841	Died During First Term	John Tyler
John Tyler	Whig	April 6, 1841	March 4, 1845	Completed Harrison's Term	Office Vacant
James K. Polk	Democrat	March 4, 1845	March 4, 1849	One	George M. Dallas
Zachary Taylor	Whig	March 5, 1849	July 9, 1850	Died During First Term	Millard Fillmore

PRESIDENTS 1–12, 1789–1850

PRESIDENT	PARTY	TOOK OFFICE	LEFT OFFICE	TERMS SERVED	VICE PRESIDENT
Millard Fillmore	Whig	July 10, 1850	March 4, 1853	Completed Taylor's Term	Office Vacant
Franklin Pierce	Democrat	March 4, 1853	March 4, 1857	One	William R.D. King
James Buchanan	Democrat	March 4, 1857	March 4, 1861	One	John C. Breckinridge
Abraham Lincoln	Republican	March 4, 1861	April 15, 1865	Served One Term, Died During Second Term	Hannibal Hamlin, Andrew Johnson
Andrew Johnson	Democrat	April 15, 1865	March 4, 1869	Completed Lincoln's Second Term	Office Vacant
Ulysses S. Grant	Republican	March 4, 1869	March 4, 1877	Two	Schuyler Colfax, Henry Wilson
Rutherford B. Hayes	Republican	March 3, 1877	March 4, 1881	One	William A. Wheeler
James A. Garfield	Republican	March 4, 1881	September 19, 1881	Died During First Term	Chester Arthur
Chester Arthur	Republican	September 20, 1881	March 4, 1885	Completed Garfield's Term	Office Vacant
Grover Cleveland	Democrat	March 4, 1885	March 4, 1889	One	Thomas A. Hendricks
Benjamin Harrison	Republican	March 4, 1889	March 4, 1893	One	Levi P. Morton
Grover Cleveland	Democrat	March 4, 1893	March 4, 1897	One	Adlai E. Stevenson
William McKinley	Republican	March 4, 1897	September 14, 1901	Served One Term, Died During Second Term	Garret A. Hobart, Theodore Roosevelt

PRESIDENT	PARTY	TOOK OFFICE	LEFT OFFICE	TERMS SERVED	VICE PRESIDENT
Theodore Roosevelt	Republican	September 14, 1901	March 4, 1909	Completed McKinley's Second Term, Served One Term	Office Vacant, Charles Fairbanks
William Taft	Republican	March 4, 1909	March 4, 1913	One	James S. Sherman
Woodrow Wilson	Democrat	March 4, 1913	March 4, 1921	Two	Thomas R. Marshall
Warren G. Harding	Republican	March 4, 1921	August 2, 1923	Died During First Term	Calvin Coolidge
Calvin Coolidge	Republican	August 3, 1923	March 4, 1929	Completed Harding's Term, Served One Term	Office Vacant, Charles Dawes
Herbert Hoover	Republican	March 4, 1929	March 4, 1933	One	Charles Curtis
Franklin D. Roosevelt	Democrat	March 4, 1933	April 12, 1945	Served Three Terms, Died During Fourth Term	John Nance Garner, Henry A. Wallace, Harry S. Truman
Harry S. Truman	Democrat	April 12, 1945	January 20, 1953	Completed Roosevelt's Fourth Term, Served One Term	Office Vacant, Alben Barkley
Dwight D. Eisenhower	Republican	January 20, 1953	January 20, 1961	Two	Richard Nixon
John F. Kennedy	Democrat	January 20, 1961	November 22, 1963	Died During First Term	Lyndon B. Johnson
Lyndon B. Johnson	Democrat	November 22, 1963	January 20, 1969	Completed Kennedy's Term, Served One Term	Office Vacant, Hubert H. Humphrey
Richard Nixon	Republican	January 20, 1969	August 9, 1974	Completed First Term, Resigned During Second Term	Spiro T. Agnew, Gerald Ford

PRESIDENT	PARTY	TOOK OFFICE	LEFT OFFICE	TERMS SERVED	VICE PRESIDENT
Gerald Ford	Republican	August 9, 1974	January 20, 1977	Completed Nixon's Second Term	Nelson A. Rockefeller
Jimmy Carter	Democrat	January 20, 1977	January 20, 1981	One	Walter Mondale
Ronald Reagan	Republican	January 20, 1981	January 20, 1989	Two	George H.W. Bush
George H.W. Bush	Republican	January 20, 1989	January 20, 1993	One	Dan Quayle
Bill Clinton	Democrat	January 20, 1993	January 20, 2001	Two	Al Gore
George W. Bush	Republican	January 20, 2001	January 20, 2009	Two	Dick Cheney
Barack Obama	Democrat	January 20, 2009			Joe Biden

"I say to you quite frankly that the time for racial discrimination is over." Jimmy Carter

WRITE TO THE PRESIDENT

You may write to the president at:

The White House
1600 Pennsylvania Avenue NW
Washington, DC 20500

You may e-mail the president at:

comments@whitehouse.gov

GLOSSARY

complex - a group of connected buildings.

dedicate - to open to public use.

Democrat - a member of the Democratic political party. Democrats believe in social change and strong government.

Democratic National Committee - a group that provides leadership for the Democratic Party.

Democratic National Convention - a national meeting held every four years during which the Democratic Party chooses its candidates for president and vice president.

draft - a system for or act of selecting individuals from a group, as for military service. People who are drafted must serve in the armed forces.

economy - the way a nation uses its money, goods, and natural resources.

embassy - the home and office of a diplomat who lives in a foreign country.

environment - all the surroundings that affect the growth and well-being of a living thing.

fraud - an act of deceiving or misrepresenting.

hostage - a person held captive by another person or group in order to make a deal with authorities.

inaugurate (ih-NAW-gyuh-rayt) - to swear into a political office.

integration - the inclusion into society of people of all races on an equal basis.

neutral - not taking sides in a conflict.

Panama Canal - a human-made, narrow canal across Panama that connects the Atlantic and Pacific oceans.

primary - a method of selecting candidates to run for public office. A political party holds an election among its own members to select the party members who will represent it in the coming general election.

Republican - a member of the Republican political party. Republicans are conservative and believe in small government.

running mate - a candidate running for a lower-rank position on an election ticket, especially the candidate for vice president.

scandal - an action that shocks people and disgraces those connected with it.

summit - a conference of highest-level officials, such as heads of government.

Vietnam War - from 1957 to 1975. A long, failed attempt by the United States to stop North Vietnam from taking over South Vietnam.

WEB SITES

To learn more about Jimmy Carter, visit ABDO Publishing Company on the World Wide Web at **www.abdopublishing.com**. Web sites about Jimmy Carter are featured on our Book Links page. These links are routinely monitored and updated to provide the most current information available.

INDEX